Contents

Some words appear in the text in bold, **like this**. You can find out what they mean by looking in the glossary.

The question of life

What is life? It might seem obvious, but what life actually is and how it works is a big question at the heart of science. We are still trying to understand how life first began, and exactly how living things work. Sometimes it's even hard to decide which things are alive and which are not.

Is it alive?

Think of a cat or dog, a tree, a germ that gives you food poisoning, a mushroom, a human being, or a spider. All these things are alive. But what about a seed? It can be stored for hundreds or even thousands of years, and then start to grow when it is put in the right conditions.

What about rivers, clouds, or lightning? They're not living things, but they are like them in many ways. They can move, grow, and change. And what about robots, or computer **viruses**? They are built to resemble living things. Like a human, a robot can take in information, decide what to do, and then do it. Computer viruses can copy themselves and spread, like real germs. Are these things just **artificial** life – or, if they are clever and complex enough, could they count as real life?

The virus mystery

A virus is a type of very tiny germ that can cause diseases. It cannot copy itself on its own, but when a virus invades living **cells**, it can reproduce and it behaves like a fully living thing. Scientists are still debating whether a virus really counts as being "alive".

Different lives

There are millions of different **species** of living things on our planet, living in many different places. Each species functions in a way that suits its surroundings. For example, a shark has **gills** and fins, which allow it to breathe and move underwater. A monkey has lungs for breathing air, and arms, legs, hands, and feet so it can get around on the ground and climb trees.

However, all living things do still have some basic things in common – such as moving, in whatever way they do it. These are what we call the seven life processes. They are: movement, respiration, sensitivity, nutrition, excretion, reproduction, and growth.

Life Processes

Anna Claybourne

www.raintreepublishers.co.uk

Visit our website to find out more information about Raintree books.

To order:

☎ Phone 0845 6044371

▤ Fax +44 (0) 1865 312263

🖳 Email myorders@raintreepublishers.co.uk

Customers from outside the UK please telephone +44 1865 312262

Raintree is an imprint of Capstone Global Library Limited, a company incorporated in England and Wales having its registered office at 7 Pilgrim Street, London, EC4V 6LB – Registered company number: 6695582

Text © Capstone Global Library Limited 2012
First published in hardback in 2012
Paperback edition first published in 2013
The moral rights of the proprietor have been asserted.

Edited by Andrew Farrow, Adrian Vigliano, and Diyan Leake
Designed by Victoria Allen
Picture research by Elizabeth Alexander
Illustrations by Oxford Design & Illustrators
Originated by Capstone Global Library Ltd
Printed in China

ISBN 978 1 406 23252 3 (hardback)
15 14 13 12 11
10 9 8 7 6 5 4 3 2 1

ISBN 978 1 406 23259 2 (paperback)
16 15 14 13 12
10 9 8 7 6 5 4 3 2 1

British Library Cataloguing in Publication Data

Claybourne, Anna.
  Life processes. -- (The web of life)
  570-dc22
A full catalogue record for this book is available from the British Library.

Acknowledgements

The author and publisher are grateful to the following for permission to reproduce copyright material: Corbis pp. 27 (© Ralph White), 31 (© Michael DeYoung); Getty Images p. 39 (Keystone-France/Gamma-Keystone); NHPA p. 23 top (Francois Gohier); Photolibrary pp. 5 (Jim R. Kohl), 9 (Richard Felber), 11 (HuntStock), 13 (Luis Javier Sandoval), 16 (Don Mason), 19 (David B. Fleetham), 23 bottom (E.A. Janes), 29 (Morales Morales), 30 (Das Fotoarchiv), 32 (Richard Clark), 35 (Kristy-Anne Glubish), 38 (Jeffrey L. Rotman), 41 (Ian Lishman); Photoshot p. 20 top (© Eye Ubiquitous); Science Photo Library pp. 15 (Power and Syred), 17 top (Adam Hart-Davis), 18 (Leonard Rue Enterprises), 24 (Wim Van Egmond, Visuals Unlimited), 25 (Scott Camazine), 28 (Biomedical Imaging Unit, Southampton General Hospital), 33 (A.B. Dowsett), 36 (Neil Bromhall), 37 (Andy Harmer); Shutterstock pp. 6 (© Igor Janicek), 8 (© Johan Swanepoel), 17 bottom (© R-photos), 20 bottom (© Birute Vijeikiene).

Cover photograph of emperor penguins in Antarctica reproduced with permission of Corbis (© Paul Souders).

Every effort has been made to contact copyright holders of material reproduced in this book. Any omissions will be rectified in subsequent printings if notice is given to the publisher.

WHAT IT MEANS FOR US

Understanding life means understanding ourselves and the other living things that share our planet. Knowing how life works lets us make medicines, develop crops, and help endangered species. One day, we might even use science to create new forms of life.

Meet Mrs Nerg

Whenever you need to remember the seven life processes, think of MRS NERG. Her name stands for:

Movement
Respiration
Sensitivity

Nutrition
Excretion
Reproduction
Growth

Imagine a strange old lady with a pet cat! Having an odd picture in your head is a good way to help you remember things.

One of the most amazing sights in the animal world – a flock of thousands of birds moving in one huge mass. These are sandpipers and dunlins in Alaska, USA.

The seven life processes

As we have seen, the seven life processes are movement, respiration, sensitivity, nutrition, excretion, reproduction, and growth. Anything that does all of these can be counted as a living thing.

What do they mean?

Each of the life processes has a particular function. This book will explain them one by one. To start with, here is a quick guide:

Movement All living things move. Animals move around, but plants and other living things can also move as they grow and change.

Respiration Respiration happens in body **cells**. It means using **oxygen** (gas) to turn food into energy. Living things take in oxygen to do this, for example by breathing. Plants respire, too (see page 14).

Sensitivity Living things sense what's around them – for example, plants and most animals can detect light.

Nutrition Nutrition means food – so this means the **organism** eats, or takes in food in some way.

Excretion An organism releases, or excretes, waste products from its blood, organs, or body tissues.

Reproduction Reproduction means having offspring or young – making new living things.

Growth All living things grow as they take in food and use it to make new cells.

The living things in this photo are engaged in several life processes: eating, using senses to detect danger, moving, and growing. Inside their cells respiration is taking place.

Creature feature: The seven life processes in a pet cat

To see the life processes in action, think of how they work in a pet cat.

- **Movement** The cat uses its muscles and joints to run, jump, lick itself, and so on.

- **Respiration** In a cat's cells, oxygen (which the cat breathes in) and food release energy.

- **Sensitivity** Cats can see, smell, and hear well, and also have senses of taste and touch.

- **Nutrition** Cats are **carnivores**. They hunt and eat meat.

- **Excretion** Cats excrete urine (waste liquid) and waste gases in their breath.

- **Reproduction** It takes a male and a female cat to make baby cats, called kittens.

- **Growth** A baby cat starts life as a single cell inside its mother's body, and grows to full size.

Alive or not?

This table shows how only living organisms have all seven life processes. Some other things may have some of them, but they are not alive.

	Cat	Cloud	Robot	Computer virus
Movement	x	x	x	x
Respiration	x			
Sensitivity	x		x	x
Nutrition	x			
Excretion	x			
Reproduction	x			x
Growth	x	x		

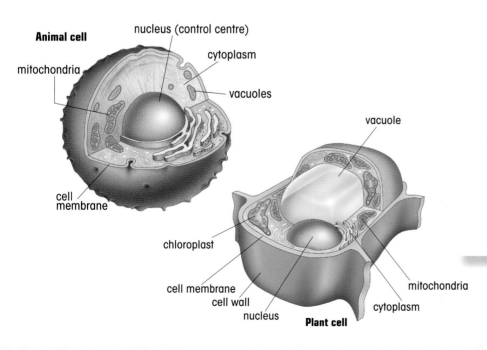

Animal cell

nucleus (control centre)

cytoplasm

mitochondria

vacuoles

cell membrane

chloroplast

cell membrane

cell wall

nucleus

Plant cell

vacuole

mitochondria

cytoplasm

All living things are made up of tiny units called cells. A large animal like a human has billions of cells, while some very small organisms such as **bacteria** are single-celled. Cells do the jobs that keep a living thing alive. They make the life processes work.

Movement

All living things move. Animals, including humans, can move around from A to B. But there are other kinds of movement too – such as flower petals opening, or blood or food moving around inside a living thing. Movement is essential. It helps living things to find, reach, and take in their food. It also happens when other life processes take place inside the body.

Different living things are **adapted** to move in different ways, depending on their surroundings and needs. A bean plant moves slowly as it grows and climbs. A frog jumps suddenly and darts its tongue out in a split second to catch a fly.

Moving bodies

Some animals, such as cats or humans, move by using a system of bones, joints, and muscles. Bones give the body shape and hold it up. Joints allow the bones to change position. Muscles are attached to the bones, and are made of **cells** that can **contract**, or shorten. As the muscles shorten, they pull on the bones. This is how we can make movements such as walking, climbing, or picking up a pen.

A gemsbok can run at almost 60 kilometres (40 miles) per hour to escape from predators such as leopards and cheetahs.

Movement methods

Different creatures have various types of body parts to help them move. Birds and insects fly with wings, and fish use their fins and tails to swim. A snail has no legs or bones, but crawls along on its single "foot", which is made up of muscles. Some tiny **bacteria** have whip-like parts called **flagella** that they swish or swivel around to push themselves along.

Plants and fungi

A plant or a mushroom may not get up and walk across the forest – but they do still move. If you leave a plant on a sunny windowsill, you'll find it gradually leans over to reach towards the light. **Fungi**, such as mushrooms, push their way up through the soil. A climbing clematis plant wraps its **tendrils** around tree twigs or fence posts to hold on tight. Daisy flowers open every morning, and a squirting cucumber fruit explodes to fling its seeds through the air.

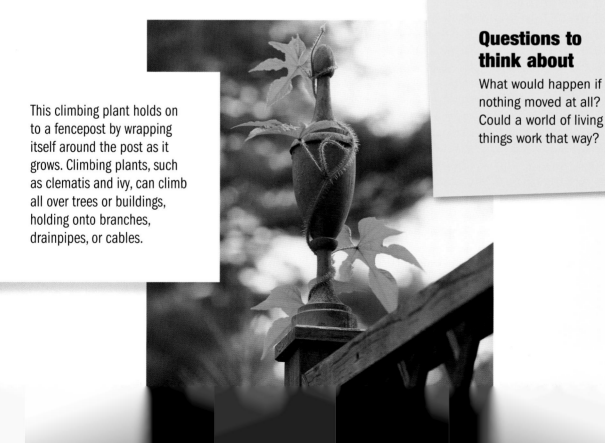

This climbing plant holds on to a fencepost by wrapping itself around the post as it grows. Climbing plants, such as clematis and ivy, can climb all over trees or buildings, holding onto branches, drainpipes, or cables.

Common confusions

Can muscles push?

Muscles cannot push, although we may feel as if we're making "pushing" movements. Muscles can only contract and pull, and then relax again. They often work in pairs to make body parts move backwards and forwards. For example, one muscle pulls your arm to bend it, and another pulls to straighten it again.

Questions to think about

What would happen if nothing moved at all? Could a world of living things work that way?

Moving inside

Besides moving your limbs around, there is also a lot of movement going on inside you. For example, your heart is always beating, and substances such as blood and food **particles** are constantly moving and flowing.

Organs and cells

Organs are body parts that do particular jobs – such as a brain, heart, or eye. To do their jobs, organs often have to move. For example, in many animals, the eye can swivel around, and its **lens** can change shape. A heart squeezes tight and relaxes with each beat. Your stomach churns and mashes food up by squeezing it with strong muscles.

Living things need to deliver things like food, water, and oxygen to all their cells, and carry waste products back out. So these things are always flowing around inside a living **organism**. In a plant, for example, water sucked through the roots is carried up through the whole plant along tubes called **xylem**. In a human, the **intestines** squeeze food along, and the heart pumps blood around the body non-stop, carrying useful chemicals. Inside the cells, the chemicals are passed to and fro and rearranged.

Body tubes, such as the oesophagus and intestines, squeeze to move things along inside them. This is called **peristalsis**.

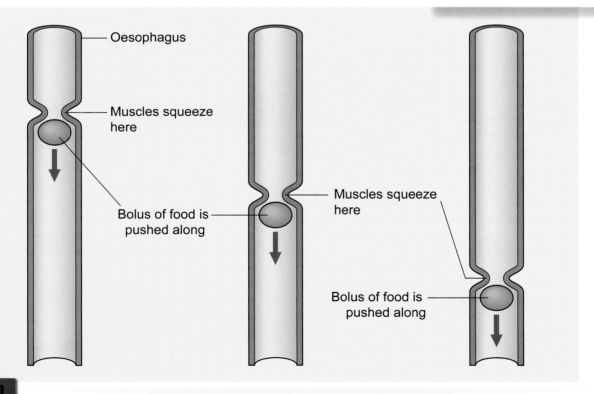

Oesophagus

Muscles squeeze here

Bolus of food is pushed along

Muscles squeeze here

Bolus of food is pushed along

Life processes

The life processes, such as growing, sensing things, taking in food, or excreting waste, depend on things being able to move inside the body. Without this movement, a living thing could not function.

Going wrong

Disease germs, drugs, and injuries can make movement difficult. For example, a broken leg or wing will not work properly. That could mean the difference between life and death for a beetle or mouse that needs to escape from a big, hungry tarantula! If you catch 'flu, your bones and muscles ache and you feel so tired you have to lie down. A bite from a blue-ringed octopus would **paralyse** your muscles, and you wouldn't be able to breathe without help.

WHAT IT MEANS FOR US

Movement allows humans to do a vast range of everyday activities – going shopping at the supermarket, eating and drinking, making friends, or building houses. However, some people have diseases or injuries that mean they can't move themselves around. They need help to do all kinds of things, such as eating, getting into a car, reading, or even talking.

Thanks to technology, we can replace some types of body parts if they go wrong or are missing. This man's artificial leg works so well, he can use it for waterskiing.

Movement and health

Moving around is good for your health. It gives your body exercise, which keeps your bones, heart, and muscles strong.

Respiration

Respiration is a **chemical reaction** that happens inside a living thing's **cells**. It combines food chemicals and **oxygen** to release energy for the living thing to use. It's essential for living things, because they need energy to power all the other life processes.

How it works

This diagram shows how respiration happens in a shark. First, oxygen and food chemicals have to get to the shark's cells to be used. They enter the shark's body as it breathes and feeds, and its blood carries them into its cells. The blood also carries away the waste products that respiration creates.

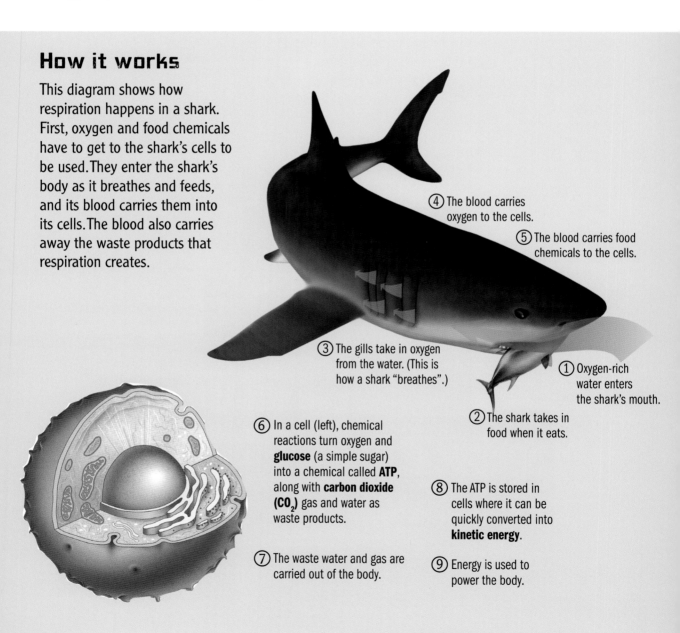

④ The blood carries oxygen to the cells.

⑤ The blood carries food chemicals to the cells.

③ The gills take in oxygen from the water. (This is how a shark "breathes".)

① Oxygen-rich water enters the shark's mouth.

② The shark takes in food when it eats.

⑥ In a cell (left), chemical reactions turn oxygen and **glucose** (a simple sugar) into a chemical called **ATP**, along with **carbon dioxide (CO$_2$)** gas and water as waste products.

⑧ The ATP is stored in cells where it can be quickly converted into **kinetic energy**.

⑦ The waste water and gas are carried out of the body.

⑨ Energy is used to power the body.

The chemical reaction can be written down like this:

Glucose + Oxygen -----> CO$_2$ + Water (+ Energy)

How gills work

Most fish get their oxygen by extracting it from the water around them through their gills. Inside the gills are lots of tiny blood vessels. As water flows past these vessels, they collect the oxygen from it and carry it into the fish's blood. At the same time, CO_2 waste passes out of the blood through the gills, and into the water.

Gills are the flap-like parts on the side of a fish's throat, as shown in this photo of a whale shark.

Common confusions

Respiration and breathing

People often confuse respiration with breathing, but it is not the same process. Respiration happens in cells, but it needs oxygen to work. Some living things get their oxygen by breathing, so breathing can play a part in respiration, but it isn't the whole story. It's important for scientists (and students!) to use the term "respiration" to mean using oxygen to produce energy, not to mean breathing.

Insect respiration

While fish have gills and mammals have lungs, insects take in oxygen through holes in their skin, called **spiracles**. Air flows into the spiracles and into tubes in the insect's body, where the oxygen is absorbed.

Respiration in plants

Respiration happens in plants, though not as much as in animals. Plants don't have muscles – they do not move around in the same way as animals, so they don't need very much energy.

How it works

Plants let air into their leaves through little holes called **stomata**. Inside the plant's cells, oxygen from the air combines with **glucose** stored in the plant. This releases energy, along with waste water and carbon dioxide, which escape back out of the leaves. The plant uses its energy to make its cells work and fuel its life processes.

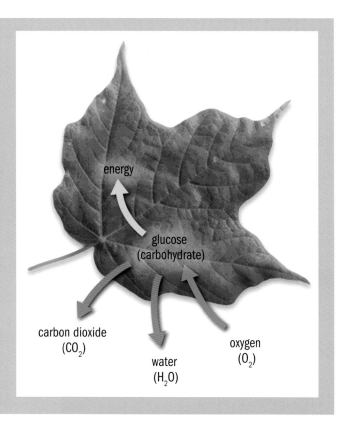

energy

glucose (carbohydrate)

carbon dioxide (CO$_2$)

water (H$_2$O)

oxygen (O$_2$)

Oxygen planet

Living things on Earth are **adapted** to work with our planet's **atmosphere** – with the oxygen in the air and in the water. They have many ways of taking in oxygen for respiration, depending on where they live and what type of creature they are.

For example, fish have gills, humans have lungs, and insects have holes called spiracles that let air into their bodies, and tubes called trachea that **absorb** the oxygen. A fish will die if it is taken out of the water, because it can only get oxygen from water using its gills. But humans can drown in water because we are only able to take oxygen from the air.

No oxygen?

Although respiration normally uses oxygen, it is possible for living things to convert food into energy without oxygen. This is called **anaerobic respiration**.

A few types of **bacteria** are adapted to live this way all the time, so they don't need oxygen. In plants and animals, it can happen sometimes when there isn't enough oxygen around. When an athlete sprints in a race, anaerobic respiration converts food into ATP to give his or her body a quick boost of energy. However, this makes the muscles sore and it only works for a short time.

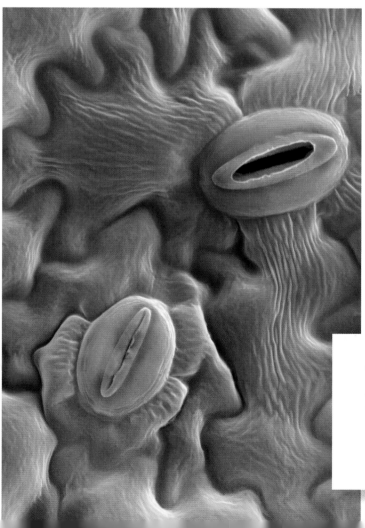

Bird breath

Birds need a huge amount of ready energy to power their flapping wings and get them off the ground. They can obtain this extra energy by taking in extra oxygen for respiration. Their lungs and breathing systems are much more efficient than ours, and get more oxygen from the air with each breath.

These strange-looking shapes are stomata on a lavender leaf, more than 1,000 times life size. They can open and close to let gases in and out of the plant.

Sensitivity

Sensitivity means sensing things and responding to them. A living **organism** senses its surroundings using its sense organs. It uses the information it collects to help it survive. For example, a snake has to use its senses to find its prey – then it strikes. Your senses tell you if food smells bad – and you avoid eating it.

Sense organs

Most humans are used to having five senses – seeing, hearing, touching, tasting, and smelling. We have sense organs for each sense – for instance, our eyes, ears, and nose. Sense organs contain special **cells** that can monitor our surroundings and send signals to the brain. For example, the back of the human eyeball contains light-detecting cells called rods and cones.

Some living things have more acute senses than humans. Dogs and bears have a much better sense of smell. A bee can see **ultraviolet** light, a blue-ish colour that we can't see.

Some creatures have other senses, too. Sharks have little jelly-filled pits around their heads called the Ampullae of Lorenzini, which can detect the faint electrical energy given off by other animals. A snake has heat pits on its face that can detect heat from other animals. Most plants have a sense of which way is down, so that they can grow upwards away from the soil.

This climber is using her sense of touch to tell when she gets a good grip on the rock, and to keep her balance. Her sense of sight also helps her find good holds.

Sensing light

For many creatures, light detection is one of the most important senses. We live on a planet bathed in light from our Sun, so living things have developed the ability to sense it. Most animals have eyes that can sense light reflected from the things around them. Plants need light to grow (see page 26) and they can sense it, too. They contain chemicals that change when light hits them, and tell the plant where the light is.

See for yourself

Look closely at your eyes in a mirror in a dimly lit room. Your pupils should look quite large, as in the first picture here, so as to let in as much light as possible to help you see. Then, turn a bright light on (or ask a friend to). Watch as your pupils shrink, so that they don't let too much light in. Your body senses how much light there is, and responds.

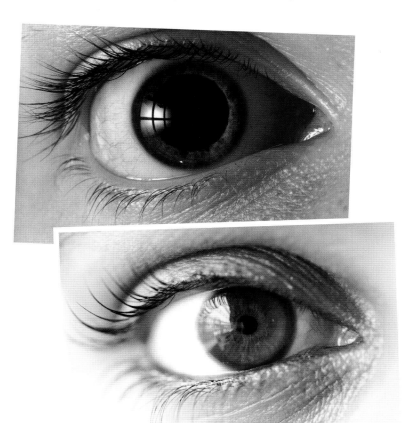

Daytime detector

Scientists have recently discovered a third type of light-sensing cell in our eyes, called the photosensitive ganglion cell. It doesn't help us see images – instead it detects light levels. This helps to control our **pupils** (see "See for yourself" text) and also our body clocks, which respond to what time of day it is and help us to wake and sleep.

Questions to think about

Do sensations feel, look, or smell the same to everyone? It's hard to tell, isn't it? Some scientists call a person's individual experiences and sensations "qualia". You cannot know exactly what other people's qualia are like!

Sensing the world

Sensitivity is essential for living things. It connects us to everything around us so we can move around, find food, communicate with others, detect danger, and make decisions.

Organisms don't just take information in – they also respond to it. This could be something you do deliberately – for example, if you see a coin on the floor, you might decide to pick it up. The cells of your **nervous system** carry sense information to your brain. Then your brain makes a decision, and sends nerve signals to your muscles.

Living things also have **reflex** responses, such as your eyes blinking if someone squirts water at them. If a lizard's tail is grabbed, its nervous system automatically discards the tail. This "amputation reflex" may allow the lizard to escape.

Hormones are chemicals released by your body to control the way it works. One example is **adrenaline**. This hormone makes your heart beat faster, sending more oxygen around your body to help you move fast. Your body automatically releases adrenaline if you sense danger.

This lava lizard has lost its tail in the past, probably by detaching it as a reflex reaction. Now it has started to grow a new tail, which isn't yet fully formed.

Communication

It is thanks to senses that living things can communicate. Squid signal to each other by using flashing patterns of colour on their skin. Humans have developed complicated languages that can communicate all sorts of information. Even **bacteria** can communicate with each other, by releasing chemicals that other bacteria can sense.

These are oval squid, a species of squid known for their brilliant colour-changing displays. They flash fast-changing patterns of rainbow colours at each other to communicate.

Am I ill?

We don't just detect things outside ourselves. Sensitivity also tells a living thing if it is injured or unwell, or if germs have invaded it. For example, if you catch a cold **virus**, your body will sense it, and your **immune system** will go to work to fight the germs.

CASE STUDY

Blue whale versus puffball fungus

Over the next four pages, you can find out about two very different creatures –
a blue whale and a puffball **fungus**. Both are living things and the seven life
processes apply to them both – but sometimes in quite different ways. By comparing
them side by side, you can see how the life processes work in the real world,
and how **organisms** in different surroundings use their life processes to survive.

The blue whale is the
biggest animal that has
ever lived. It's a mammal
and breathes air, but it
lives in the sea and can
dive deep under water.

Common confusions

Fungi and plants

Fungi, such as the common
puffball and other mushrooms
and toadstools, are not plants.
Though they grow in the soil like
plants, they do not use sunshine
to make food, as plants do. They
feed on rotting plant and animal
matter in the soil, releasing
chemicals that break it down
into a liquid, then soaking it
up into their cells.

The puffball fungus is a type of
mushroom. It belongs to the fungi
family of living things, along with
toadstools, moulds, and yeast.

Compare the creatures

	Blue whale	Common puffball
	The blue whale is a mammal (a type of animal) that lives in the sea.	The puffball is a mushroom (a type of fungus) found in woodlands and fields.
Movement	The blue whale is a **vertebrate** with a skeleton and muscles. It powers itself through the water with its huge tail.	The puffball's **mycelium** (a root-like network of very fine threads) spreads underground. The large, ball-shaped **fruiting body** grows above ground, sometimes exploding to disperse **spores**.
Respiration	A blue whale has lungs and breathes in air to collect oxygen from it. Oxygen is carried in its blood to the cells where respiration releases energy from food.	The puffball fungus takes oxygen into cells in its mycelium, where the process of respiration converts food into energy.
Sensitivity	Blue whales have a very good sense of hearing, and communicate with each other using very deep calling noises. They also have a good sense of touch. They can't smell especially well, but can taste and may also be able to sense the Earth's magnetic field.	The fungus can detect food and moisture, allowing it to feed and grow its fruiting body (the puffball) at times when it will survive best. It cannot see, hear, smell, or think, as it has no brain.

Compare the creatures

	Blue whale	Common puffball
Nutrition	Blue whales have **baleen** in their mouths – plates of a fingernail-like substance that can sieve the water to catch small creatures such as **krill** and **plankton** (see picture top right).	The puffball **absorbs** and feeds on rotting plant and animal material in damp soil. Its mycelium spreads out underground to reach as much food as possible.
Excretion	Like a human, the whale **excretes** waste through its lungs and kidneys. It also excretes any excess salt that enters its body from the sea water.	A common puffball excretes waste gases from the process of respiration.
Reproduction	To reproduce, a male and a female whale mate and the baby grows in the female's body. Like all mammals, mother whales feed their young on milk from their bodies.	The puffball grows millions of very small seed-like parts, called spores, which it "puffs" out into the air in a cloud when it is touched or knocked (see picture bottom right). The spores float away and can grow into new fungi where they land.
Growth	A blue whale grows from a single cell inside its mother. At birth it is about 7.5 metres (nearly 25 feet) long, and when it reaches adult size it can be up to 33 metres (108 feet) long – the world's biggest animal.	The puffball's mycelium grows as it spreads out below the ground. The fruiting body, the puffball itself, grows to about 6 centimetres (just over 2 inches) across and 9 centimetres (3.5 inches) high.

The baleen filters inside a whale's mouth let water through, but catch the tiny creatures that are the whale's food.

Life on Earth

As the two examples in this case study show, living things can vary enormously in size, appearance, lifestyle, and the ways in which their life processes work. Scientists have already discovered and named around 2 million **species** of living things, but new ones are constantly being found. In fact, there may be many more millions of living things that we have not yet discovered.

Questions to think about

How might climate change impact on the life processes and survival of these two living organisms? Could they be affected by rising sea levels, rising temperatures, changes in weather, or a different balance of gases in the **atmosphere**?

When it is ripe, a puffball "puffs" its tiny spores into the air in a fine cloud.

Nutrition

Nutrition means food, and all living things need food. They use **nutrients**, or food chemicals, for energy and growth, to keep body parts working, and to repair injuries.

Eating and feeding

Living things take in their nutrition in various ways. Most animals eat with a mouth. It can be a mouth with biting jaws and teeth, such as the mouth of a human, a dog, or a shark. Some animals have straw-shaped sucking mouths, like a fly's **proboscis**. Some, like birds and octopuses, have beaks. Some single-**celled** animals, such as **amoebas**, simply wrap themselves around their food and **absorb** it.

Plants take in nutrients from the soil through their roots, but they also get food by converting energy from sunlight into nutrients (see page 26).

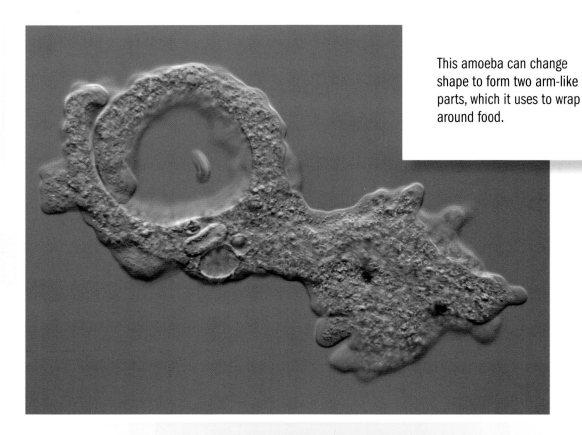

This amoeba can change shape to form two arm-like parts, which it uses to wrap around food.

Digestive systems

Many living things have digestive systems that break down the food they eat into the chemicals they need. In humans, the food goes into the stomach, then through the **intestines** where it is liquidized and broken down by chemicals called **enzymes**. Then the food chemicals are absorbed by the intestine wall and transferred into the blood, which carries them to where they are needed.

Digestion doesn't actually have to happen inside the body. **Fungi** release digestive enzymes on to their food to dissolve it, before soaking it up into their **cells**. Some starfish stick their stomach out through their mouth and insert it into the shell of their shellfish prey. They then digest the animal's soft body before sucking the stomach back in.

In this X-ray you can see a human stomach (in yellow) and small intestine (in pink). The small intestine is tightly coiled up, but if it were stretched out it would be as long as a classroom!

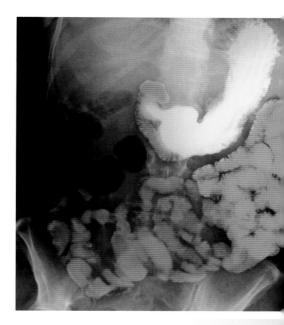

WHAT IT MEANS FOR US

We don't just need food – we need the right types of food. For humans, a healthy diet is a good balance of food types: protein, fat, carbohydrates, fibre, vitamins, and minerals. These foods provide the chemicals our cells and tissues need to support all our life processes. Without a balanced diet, we can become ill. For example, a lack of vitamin C can lead to a disease called scurvy, which causes tiredness, weakness, blotchy skin, and rotten teeth.

Waste

The parts of food that are not needed leave a living thing's body as waste. As an earthworm burrows through the ground, soil moves right through its body. It extracts the nutrients it needs from the soil, and the rest comes out as waste. Some **carnivores**, such as owls and komodo dragons, eat their prey whole and then regurgitate (sick up) some of the waste bits (fur, claws, and bones) in a lump or pellet.

Plant food

Plants feed in a different way from other living things. Most living things are **heterotrophs**, which means they feed on other living things. Plants are **autotrophs**, which means they make their own food. They do this using light, in a process called **photosynthesis**.

How does photosynthesis work?

Photosynthesis happens when a plant absorbs sunlight into its leaves, and uses the light energy to power a chemical reaction between water sucked up through its roots and **carbon dioxide (CO_2)** from the air. The reaction takes place inside the parts of the leaf's cells called **chloroplasts**. It produces oxygen and water, which are expelled from the leaf, and sugar chemicals that the plant uses as food.

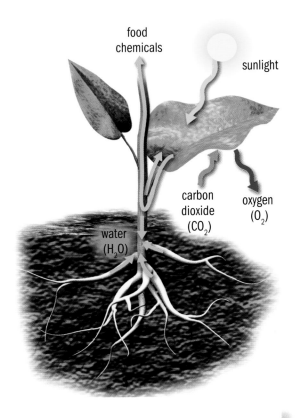

food chemicals

sunlight

carbon dioxide (CO_2)

oxygen (O_2)

water (H_2O)

This diagram shows how photosynthesis happens inside a leaf.

Food chains

Nutrition gives a living thing the energy it needs to live. As some **organisms** eat other organisms, food energy is taken from one creature to the next, in a sequence called a **food chain**. Food chains start with plants, which take in energy from the Sun. The energy passes on to animals that eat plants, and then to animals that eat those animals, and so on. Because of this, almost all life depends on photosynthesis. If plants did not use sunlight to make food, there would be no food for plant-eating animals, or for the animals that eat those animals – and that means no food for us.

Hydrothermal vents are places on the seabed, where hot, mineral-filled water escapes. There, bacteria that don't use sunlight provide food for giant tubeworms, like these.

Sunlight into food

Plants are often described as "making food" out of sunlight, which sounds confusing. What this means is that the Sun's energy is used to make other ingredients react together. This creates new chemicals that are carried around inside the plant, and used to grow and build new plant parts.

Life without light

Most food energy comes from sunlight, via plants. But there are some living things that don't depend on sunlight. Some of the **archaea** (a type of single-celled organism) use chemicals such as ammonia or hydrogen to turn food into energy. They form the basis of their own food chains, separate from plant-based ones. It is possible that if other forms of life exist beyond our planet, some could use similar, non-light-based ways of making food.

Excretion

Excretion happens when a living thing gets rid of waste products from its blood, organs, or body tissues. The waste is made during other life processes, such as respiration. It is a result of **metabolism** – the chemical reactions that happen in a living thing to allow it to survive.

It's important to get rid of waste, but excretion can sometimes have other useful functions, too. Some living things have adapted to use their excretions to help them in other ways.

What kind of waste?

One of the main types of excretion is the removal of waste gases made during respiration (see page 12). Respiration happens in **cells**, so the waste **carbon dioxide (CO_2)** gas and water it produces have to be carried out of the **organism** to be released. In humans, they come out through the lungs, as we breathe out. In plants, they escape through **stomata** (tiny holes) in the leaves.

Other types of excretion include sweat and urine. Sweat carries excess water and waste chemicals (especially salt) out of tiny holes, or **pores**, in the skin. Urine also removes excess water, along with waste chemicals from the blood. Urine is produced by the kidneys, which constantly filter all the blood in the body and remove the waste.

This is a human sweat pore, one of the openings in the skin that sweat escapes from. It is shown over 300 times larger than life size.

Useful excretions

Sweat is an example of an excretion that serves another useful purpose, besides carrying out waste. It makes our skin wet, and this helps us to cool down in hot weather. A little sweat can also give our hands and feet a better grip for climbing and holding things.

Urine has other uses too. Animals such as dogs use it for marking their territory, as other animals can smell it. We even use human and animal urine to make some types of medicines, and as part of the process of making leather and some fabrics.

Common confusions

Excretion and egestion

The word *excretion* is sometimes used to mean the process of getting rid of **faeces**. In fact, the removal of faeces is not true excretion. Faeces do not come from the body's metabolism, but are simply separated food waste. The correct name for the removal of food waste is **egestion**.

The white crust on this marine iguana's nose is made from excretions of sea salt.

Sneezing lizard

The marine iguana is an unusual lizard that lives in and around the sea on the Galapagos Islands in the Pacific Ocean. Its body absorbs salt from the seawater. It has a special gland on its nose that excretes excess salt by sneezing it out. This gives the iguana a crusty white patch on its face.

Staying the same

Excretion is very important for living things because it helps them keep their bodies in a balanced, healthy state, called **homeostasis**. Homeostasis simply means "staying the same". Water levels, salt levels, and the amount of sugar in the blood need to be kept fairly constant for the body to stay healthy.

As food and water enter the body, and life processes create waste products, the leftover and waste material has to be removed. Otherwise it would collect and build up in the body. A living thing with too much water in its body, or a build-up of waste chemicals, would not be able to function properly and would become ill or die.

Using excretions

Humans have found ways to use some of the excretions of other living things to our advantage. One important example is yeast. It's a type of single-celled **fungus** that lives in groups, or colonies. As yeast feeds on sugar chemicals, it excretes waste CO_2. By mixing yeast with sugar and adding it to drinks and bread dough, we can capture the bubbles of CO_2. This is what puts the fizz into drinks such as beer, and creates the bubbles in bread dough that make it rise.

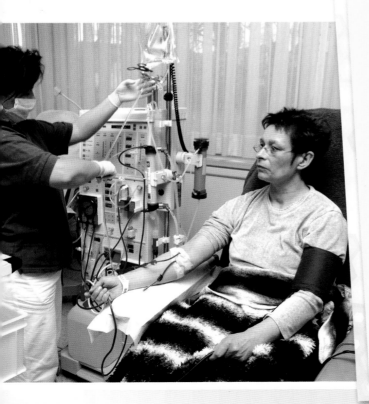

WHAT IT MEANS FOR US

You can appreciate how important urine is when you think about what could happen if your kidneys stop working. If your kidneys could not remove waste from your body in the normal way, poisonous chemicals would start to collect in your blood. These dangerous poisons can cause illness and death. Several times a week you would need to have your blood cleaned by a special **dialysis** machine that does the job of the kidneys. People with kidney failure are sometimes offered a kidney transplant, when a healthy kidney is donated from someone else – but this can also bring problems. For instance, the body can reject and fight against the new organ.

See for yourself

When it's very cold, you can see your own breath. If you breathe on to a cold surface, such as a window, it will become cloudy from the waste water droplets you are breathing out. This happens because your lungs excrete water, a waste product of respiration, as water vapour (water gas).

On a cold day, your breath can look like a cloud in the air. The water vapour from your lungs condenses into small water droplets that you can see as a white-ish cloud when the air is very cold.

Reproduction

Reproduction means making new things that are the same as the original. Living things reproduce by making new living things that are the same **species** as themselves. Having babies is one kind of reproduction, but there are others, too. Reproduction can be divided into two main types.

Sexual reproduction

In **sexual reproduction**, a male and a female **cell** from two living things of the same species join together. They combine to make a new cell that can grow into a new living thing – a baby, young, or offspring. For example, when a male and a female elephant mate, the male passes **sperm cells** (male reproductive cells) into the female's body. There, a sperm cell combines with an **egg cell** (a female reproductive cell). They form a new cell, which grows into a baby elephant inside its mother before being born.

This is a Highland cow with her calf. Like all mammals, cows use sexual reproduction. The calf grows from two cells, one from its father and one from its mother, after they join together.

Asexual reproduction

Asexual reproduction does not require two living things or two different cells. There is only one parent, and it makes exact copies of itself, by copying its own cells. This can happen in single-celled creatures, such as **bacteria**, that reproduce by dividing in two. Each new cell is a copy of the first, and can also divide in two. Some larger creatures can also reproduce asexually. For example, a water animal called the hydra grows a "bud", or smaller copy of itself, which eventually breaks away from its parent.

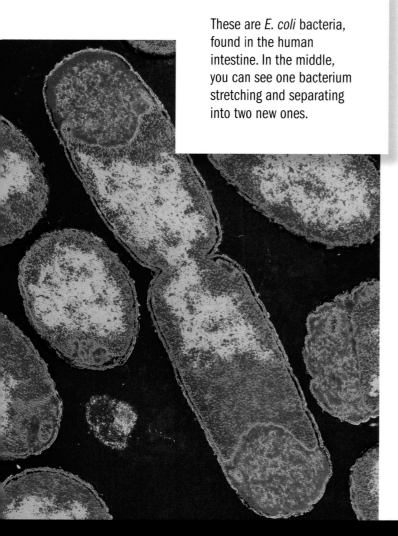

These are *E. coli* bacteria, found in the human intestine. In the middle, you can see one bacterium stretching and separating into two new ones.

Common confusions

When two cells meet

Sexual reproduction isn't just about mating. It simply means a male and a female cell joining. This doesn't always happen inside the bodies of living things. For example, some fish release their sperm and egg cells into the water, and they meet and combine there, becoming embryos that later hatch from the egg as baby fish. Human "test-tube" embryos are created from male and female reproductive cells that have been collected from the parents and combined in a laboratory.

Strange snails

Common snails are pretty unusual when it comes to reproduction. There are no male or female snails – each individual is both male and female. When they mate, they share their male and female reproductive cells. Both the snails then get pregnant and lay eggs in the soil. The eggs hatch out into baby snails.

WORD BANK
sexual reproduction   reproduction from the combination of a male and a female cell
asexual reproduction   reproduction from copying a single parent's cells

Plant reproduction

Most plants reproduce sexually. Flowers are a plant's reproductive organs. They have parts called **anthers** that release **pollen** cells (male reproductive cells). These travel on the wind, or are carried around by animals such as bees, until they land on another flower of the same species. There, a pollen cell joins on to the female flower parts, and a pollen tube grows down inside the flower to meet a female egg cell. This creates a seed that can grow into a new plant.

Many plants can reproduce asexually, too. For example, a single strawberry plant sends out stalks called runners. The runners land in the soil, put down roots, and eventually become new, separate strawberry plants.

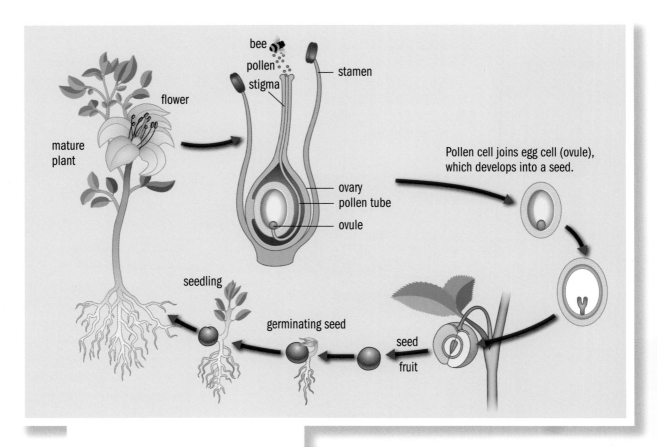

This diagram shows how flowering plants reproduce.

Passing on DNA

Deoxyribonucleic Acid (DNA) is a substance found inside cells of living things. Patterns in the DNA act as a code that tells each species how to live and grow, and what form to take. When a living thing reproduces, its DNA is copied into the cells used to make the offspring. This is why offspring are always the same species as their parents – because they have the same DNA. DNA also carries codes for particular variations in a species, such as a long nose, hair or fur colour, strength, and so on.

See for yourself

Look at yourself and your family members, or friends and their parents and siblings, to see if you can spot features that have been passed on in DNA. Can you find facial features, hair colour, tallness, or shortness that seem to run in a family?

Nature's clones

Clones are not just found in sci-fi films – some types of clones are all around us. When living things reproduce sexually, the offspring is not identical to its parents. It is made from cells from both of them, and so contains a combination of slightly different DNA patterns from each parent.

But in asexual reproduction, the offspring is a clone of its parent. A clone simply means an exact copy, with exactly the same DNA. The parent's DNA is copied and passed on in the cells used to make the offspring. When an **organism** such as a strawberry plant or hydra reproduces asexually, the offspring are all clones.

Identical twins share exactly the same DNA, so they are just like clones.

WORD BANK

deoxyribonucleic acid (DNA)   chemical found in cells that stores coded instructions for how a living thing grows and lives

clone   living thing that is an exact copy of another living thing and has the same DNA

Growth

All living things grow. Growing not only means getting bigger and bigger – but also growing hair and fingernails, as well as new body parts as you get older. Every year plants grow new parts, such as leaves, buds, and flowers, and keep growing throughout their lives.

Growing up

Living things start life as single **cells** or small parts of their parents' bodies. They get bigger and bigger until they reach the right size for their **species**, and are able to have young themselves. An **organism** grows by taking in food, or **nutrients** (see page 24). While some food is used for energy, some is turned into body substances and tissues that become part of the living thing.

This photo shows a human fetus (unborn baby) growing inside its mother's womb. The tube-shaped part on the right is the umbilical cord. It carries food from the mother to the fetus so that it can grow.

New cells

Living things grow by making more and more cells, building a bigger and bigger body. To make more cells, existing cells divide into two. Each new cell takes in nutrients and grows to the same size as the original cell. However, not all cells do this. Some cells, such as your blood cells, are made by other parts of the body. They constantly die off and have to be replaced.

Population growth

If **bacteria** get into food that's been left in a warm place, we say that they are "growing". But the individual bacteria do not grow bigger. Instead, the number of bacteria increases as they keep dividing and multiplying, so you end up with millions of bacteria instead of just a few. So long as there is enough food and the right conditions, the population (total number) of most living things will keep growing.

Questions to think about

Do you think life would be better for humans as a species if we were a lot bigger – or a lot smaller? Have you ever wondered why we don't keep growing until we're really huge?

A new skin

Some creatures, such as insects, spiders, and crabs, go through several different stages, or **instars**, as they grow from a baby to an adult. They have a tough outer skin or shell, called an **exoskeleton**, which cannot stretch and grow. So as the animal gets bigger, it must break out of its old skin and shed it. The animal then emerges with a new exoskeleton that soon hardens.

The emperor dragonfly in this photo is leaving its old instar skin behind.

How big?

Most living things and their body parts reach a maximum size for their species as they reach adulthood – they don't keep growing forever. Each species has developed to be able to survive and find food at a particular size.

Body type and the **ecosystem** that a species lives in also affect how big it can be. For example, **invertebrates** (animals without backbones) normally don't grow very large, because they have no skeleton inside them to hold up a heavy body, and their respiratory system cannot deliver enough oxygen to power a large animal. So even the biggest insects and spiders are only about the size of a dinner plate.

In the sea, where the water can support their bodies, invertebrates can grow bigger. Here there are giant squid, spider crabs with a leg span as long as a car, and jellyfish that are bigger than humans.

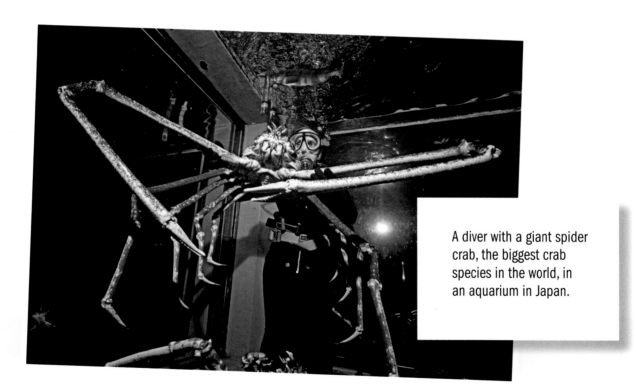

A diver with a giant spider crab, the biggest crab species in the world, in an aquarium in Japan.

Prehistoric giants

In prehistoric times, some types of living things were bigger than they are now. There were monster-sized sharks, dragonflies, and sloths. There were also dinosaurs, giant reptiles far bigger than any alive today. This was partly because there was more oxygen in the air and a plentiful food supply.

Limited growth

Many factors can affect how a living thing grows. If organisms don't get enough healthy nutrients as they are growing up, they can end up smaller than average. Diseases sometimes make a living thing stop growing properly. Some types of drugs can affect the development of unborn babies, making them grow in unusual ways.

There are also **hormones** that affect how big or small an organism grows. The tallest man ever recorded was Robert Wadlow. He grew to 2.72 metres (8 feet 11 inches) because of problems with his growth hormones. Being so big also affected Wadlow's life processes – for example, he had very little sensation in his feet.

The biggest living things

The biggest plant is the giant sequoia tree. It can be 90 metres (295 feet) tall and weigh 1,180 tonnes. The biggest animal ever to have lived is the blue whale. It can grow to 33 metres (108 feet) long and weigh over 130 tonnes. The biggest living thing of all is not known for certain, but it may be a type of underground **fungus**.

Robert Wadlow, born in the United States in 1918, was the tallest human ever recorded.

A world of life

As you can see, the seven life processes are vital for the survival of all living things, and all living things have them. The life processes are not separate – they work together in an **organism**, and are linked and interconnected. They also connect living things to one another, as they feed on each other, take in each other's waste gases, communicate, and rely on each other.

Processes in a cycle

For example, for the process of respiration to happen in **cells**, a living thing has to take in food – the process of nutrition. It has to use sensitivity to find food, and movement to reach it. Respiration and feeding lead to the process of excretion. To power all these processes, an organism needs energy – and this is provided by respiration. Energy also powers reproduction, which allows a **species** to continue existing over time.

Life is everywhere

All the life processes are going on constantly, inside us and all around us. For example, at this moment, **bacteria** are growing on your teeth, dogs are barking, someone is heading a football, butterfly eggs are nestled on a leaf waiting to hatch, houseplants are exchanging gases with the air around them, and insects are buzzing about in classrooms. When you eat your lunch, run for the bus, laugh at a funny film, or blink when someone switches on your bedroom light, your life processes are playing their parts.

See for yourself

When you do various daily activities, think about which life processes they involve.

For example:

- cleaning your teeth
- whistling
- eating an apple
- reading a book
- playing a ball game
- checking the weather to see what to wear
- running to catch a bus
- going to the toilet
- chatting to your mum
- using a computer to contact a friend
- falling asleep

Questions to think about

Can you imagine a living thing that didn't have all the life processes that living things on Earth do? Could it exist without movement, or without respiration, sensitivity, nutrition, excretion, reproduction, or growth? If it could, what might it be like? Could alien species from beyond Earth work differently and have different life processes?

At any moment in your everyday life, you'll be surrounded by life processes.

Life processes at a glance

These two pages contain a quick reminder of all the life processes and what they mean. Don't forget to use "Mrs Nerg" to help you remember what they are!

	Meaning	Examples
Movement	· Moving; whether that means walking from A to B, plants moving petals and stems as they grow, or movement inside a living thing.	· Fish using their tails to swim. · Moving our mouths to chew and talk. · Slime mould spreading across the ground. · A seed pod popping open.
Respiration	· Taking in oxygen and using it in body cells to help convert food chemicals into energy for the living things to use.	· Humans taking oxygen from the air into the lungs, and carrying it to cells in the blood. · Plants taking in oxygen through leaves for respiration in leaf cells.
Sensitivity	· Sensing the surroundings by seeing them, hearing them, feeling them, or in other ways, and responding to what is detected.	· Squid using skin patterns to signal to one another. · A plant sensing a source of light. · A rattlesnake detecting body heat from its prey.

	Meaning	Examples
Nutrition	· Eating or taking in food to provide the living thing with energy and the chemicals it needs to grow.	· Tigers hunting and eating other animals, such as deer. · Fungi soaking up food chemicals from their surroundings. · Plants converting sunlight into food energy using **photosynthesis**.
Excretion	· Collecting and releasing waste products from the body, such as waste gases, chemicals, and liquids.	· Human kidneys filtering excess water and waste chemicals from the blood. · A plant releasing oxygen from its leaves as a waste product of photosynthesis.
Reproduction	· Making babies or offspring – new living things that are the same species (or type of organism) as their parents.	· A single-celled organism splitting in two to make two new copies of itself. · A male and female swan mating, and the female laying eggs that hatch into babies. · Apple trees making seeds in their fruit that can then grow into new apple trees.
Growth	· Growing, including a living thing growing bigger as it gets older, and growing new body parts.	· A human growing from a baby into an adult. · A plant growing new leaves, buds, flowers, and fruit as the seasons change. · A deer growing new antlers every year. · An insect growing a new skin and shedding its old one as it gets bigger.

Glossary

absorb soak up

adapt change over time to become more suitable

adrenaline hormone that makes the body ready for action

amoeba a tiny, single-celled living thing

anaerobic respiration respiration without oxygen

anther part of a flower that makes and releases pollen cells

archaea single-celled living things that can live in extreme environments

artificial made by humans to replace something natural

asexual reproduction reproduction from copying a single parent's cells

atmosphere layer of gases surrounding the Earth

ATP chemical that contains energy ready to use

autotroph living thing, such as a plant, that makes its own food

bacterium (plural: **bacteria**) type of single-celled living thing

baleen plates in a whale's mouth that filter food from the water

carbon dioxide (CO_2) gas found in the air and released as waste by body cells

carnivore living thing that eats meat

cell building block of living things, and the smallest unit of life

chemical reaction change that happens when two or more substances are combined and turn into different substances

chloroplast unit inside plant cells in which photosynthesis takes place

clone living thing that is an exact copy of another living thing and has the same DNA

contract shorten or tighten

dialysis artificial filtering of the blood to remove waste

deoxyribonucleic acid (DNA) chemical found in cells that stores coded instructions for how a living thing grows and lives

ecosystem surroundings that an organism lives in

egestion removal of food waste from the body

egg cell female reproductive cell

enzyme chemical that breaks down other chemicals

excrete to push out waste from the body

exoskeleton tough outer shell or skin of some types of living things

faeces food waste expelled from the body

flagella whip-shaped body parts

food chain sequence of living things, each feeding on the one before

fruiting body part of a mushroom or toadstool that appears above ground

fungus (plural: **fungi**) type of living thing that includes mushrooms and moulds

gills organs that fish and some other water creatures use to extract oxygen from water

glucose type of simple sugar chemical

heterotroph living thing that feeds on other living things

homeostasis state of balance in a living thing

hormone body chemical that controls how a living thing works

immune system body system that fights disease

instars stages of growth in some animals, such as insects

intestine tube-shaped body part that carries food through the body and soaks up useful chemicals

invertebrate animal without a backbone

kinetic energy movement energy

krill small shrimp-like sea creatures

lens transparent part of the eye that collects and focuses light

mycelium thread-like network that forms the underground part of a mushroom

metabolism chemical reactions that happen in a living thing to allow it to survive

nervous system body system that senses things and carries messages around the body

nutrient food chemical

organism any kind of living thing

oxygen a gas found in the air

paralyse make something unable to move

particle tiny part of something

peristalsis the way some tube-shaped body parts can squeeze things along inside them

photosynthesis process plants use to make food using light energy from the Sun

plankton tiny organisms that float around in water

pollen male plant reproductive cells

pore tiny hole in the skin for excreting substances

proboscis long, narrow body part on a living thing's head, usually a type of mouth

pupil small round hole in the centre of an eye

reflex automatic response

sexual reproduction reproduction from the combination of a male and a female cell

species basic category of biological classification, composed of related individuals that are able to breed amongst themselves but not with other species

sperm cell male reproductive cell

spiracle hole in an insect's body that lets air in

spore tiny seed-like part released by fungi

stomata tiny holes in plant leaves that let air in

tendril part of a plant that coils around objects

ultraviolet type of blue-ish light not visible to humans

vertebrate animal with a backbone

virus type of tiny germ

xylem tubes that carry water around inside plants

Find out more

Books

Animal Cells and Life Processes, Barbara Somervill (Raintree, 2010)

Cells and Life Processes (Science Essentials), Denise Walker (Evans Brothers, 2010)

Experiments with Plants and Other Living Things, Trevor Cook (Franklin Watts, 2009)

Food Relationships and Webs (Living Processes), Carol Ballard (Wayland, 2009)

Life, Michael Gunton and Martha Holmes (BBC Books, 2009)

Life Cycles (Living Processes), Richard Spilsbury (Wayland, 2009)

Plant Cells and Life Processes, Barbara Somervill (Raintree, 2010)

The Scientists Behind Living Things (Sci-Hi), Robert Snedden (Raintree, 2011)

Websites

BBC KS3 Bitesize
**www.bbc.co.uk/schools/ks3bitesize/science/organisms_behaviour
_health/life_processes/revise1.shtml**
Revision notes and key points on the seven life processes.

Biology4Kids
www.biology4kids.com
Detailed, wide-ranging information on many aspects of life science.

Oxford University Museum of Natural History: The Learning Zone – Animals
www.oum.ox.ac.uk/thezone/animals/life/index.htm
An introduction to the seven life processes.

Science Resources: Life Processes and Cells
**www.science-resources.co.uk/KS3/Biology/Life_Processes_and_
Cells/Life_processes.htm**
Useful facts on life processes and living things.

Topics to research

How have humans changed?

Has the average height and weight of a human changed through history? If so, why? What changes do we have to make in our lives if we change size? Think about things such as aircraft seats, doorways, and clothes sizes.

Life on other planets

Has any evidence been found to suggest that life may exist beyond our planet? If it has, what kind of living things might exist there? Find out about extremophiles and consider whether they could survive on other planets. On balance, do you think it's likely that aliens do exist somewhere?

How it all began

Can you find out how scientists think life first started? What is the earliest type of living thing known to science?

Artificial life

Find out about the latest robots and artificial intelligence software. What do you think are the differences between a natural living thing and artificial life? One day, will artificial life become so real that we cannot tell the difference?

Index